Betty

GW00806404

Mother's Whispers Breaking the Chain

Poetry and Short Stories

Keep Up Your Prayers, God Sees God Knows, and God always carry us through Amen

Maggie Heston

Part proceeds from this book going to the Thomasadam Charity

This book is based on real life experiences, people that Maggie has met over the years that inspired her and her strong faith and belief.

Maggie

To order additional copies of this book, contact:
Xlibris LLC
0-800-056-3182
www.xlibrispublishing.co.uk
Orders@xlibrispublishing.co.uk
307333

Contents

Acknowledgement

This book is dedicated to my father, James Heston (RIP), my wonderful mother, Bridget, and my sons, Michael, Denis, and Patrick for all your love, patience, and support. A special thank you to all who supported me and worked so hard with me in getting this book published. You know who ye are.

Maggie Heston

Homestead by the Sea

Last night I went down memory lane, just as I closed my eyes,
To a little cottage by the sea, in the heart of Ballycroy
Fond memories, I will keep with me until the day I die
For in that family home, eleven children laughed and cried
Blessed with loving parents, who always showed they cared
We never wanted for anything, though times back then were hard
Each and every one of us, we surely played our part
From keeping our little cottage clean, to harnessing the horse and cart
Periwinkles, they were gathered, the turf, it was piled high
The haystack standing proudly, sure, I thought it reached the sky
The Atlantic was our swimming pool, no boundaries did we know
Our cinema was when the sun went down and the sea lions put on a show
Father led the rosary, while Mother stirred the pot, and all of its ingredients
Came from our little garden plot
The sound of music filled the air as Dad's hand strolled along the keys
The red and white melodeon sitting proudly on his knees
We danced around the kitchen floor, 'til our eyelids felt like lead
Then one by one we trotted off, to find the best place in the bed
Just as we nodded off, to the sound of the waves break on the shore
A loving kiss from Mom and Dad, sure we couldn't ask for more
Next morning as I woke, I realised it was just a dream
Precious childhood memories of our homestead in Dooriel

Many changes may have happened within our family fold and we have all parted
To seek our fortunes, all around the globe
All grown up and settled now, with families of our own
Every now and then we wander back, to where we used to be
That little piece of Heaven, our Homestead by the Sea

Maggie Heston
March 2010

Memories of my wonderful childhood, a special thank you to my parents that made it possible for my children to share those memories too.

A Special Gift

For four generations they have done the rounds, I'm proud to say now
they are mine.
Passed down through the years, shrouded with faith, love and probably
laughter and tears.
When I hold them, all my fears disappear, in my weakest moments I'm never
alone, because I'm reminded of God's heavenly throne.
As my fingers travel from bead to bead, my heart follows the one that leads.
At the end of the day, before I go to sleep, I lay them down gently within
my reach.
I'm not talking about riches and gold, it's about my mother's love.
For the special gift that's been passed down to me, is just a simple pair of
rosary beads.
On them thousands of rosaries said, and I'm sure most of those prayers
were heard.
For all of the riches this world can give, nothing fulfils my heart more
than this.
For when it is my time to pass on my beads, I know they will ease my
children's grief.
And they in turn will pray on the beads, and our lady will tend to all of their
needs

Our lady's words to the world, pray the rosary it saves our souls.
It's never too late for us to start, just pick up the beads and pray from the
heart.

01/03/2013

The most precious gift parents can give to their children is faith, and one of
the symbols of our faith is the rosary beads.

The Rosary

1. Make the sign of the cross and say the Creed
2. Say the Our Father
3. Say the three Hail Marys and the Glory Be
4. Name the first mystery and your intentions and then the Our Father
5. Say the ten Hail Marys while you're thinking of the mystery
6. Say the Glory Be (optional—after each decade, say the Fatima prayer)
7. Name the second mystery and your intentions, then say the Our Father, repeat five, six, and seven
8. Say the Hail Holy Queen when the five decades are completed

Let us Pray

The Creed

I believe in God, the Father Almighty, creator of heaven and earth. I believe in Jesus Christ, his only Son, our Lord, who was conceived by the Holy Spirit, born of the Virgin Mary, suffered under Pontius Pilate, was crucified, died and was buried. He descended to the dead. On the third day he arose again. He ascended in to heaven, is seated at the right hand of the Father. He shall come again to judge the living and the dead. I believe in the Holy Spirit, the Holy Catholic Church, communion of saints, the forgiveness of sins, the resurrection of the Body, and life everlasting. Amen.

Our Father

Our Father, who art in heaven, Hallowed be thy name. Thy kingdom come, thy will be done on earth as it is in Heaven. Give us this day our daily bread, and forgive us our trespasses as we forgive those who trespass against us and lead us not in to temptation, but deliver us from evil. Amen.

Glory Be to the Father

Glory be to the Father and to the Son and to the Holy Spirit, as it was in the beginning, is now and ever shall be, world without end. Amen.

Let us Pray

Hail Mary

Hail Mary, full of grace, the Lord is with thee. Blessed art thou amongst woman, and blessed is the fruit of thy womb, Jesus. Holy Mary, Mother of God, Pray for us sinners, now and at the hour of our death. Amen.

Fatima Prayer

O my Jesus, forgive us our sins, save us from the fires of Hell; lead all souls to Heaven, especially those who are in most need of your mercy.

Hail Holy Queen

Hail, Holy Queen, Mother of mercy, Hail our life, our sweetness and our hope! To thee do we cry, poor banished children of eve, to thee do we send up or sighs, mourning and weeping in this valley of tears. Turn then, most gracious advocate, thine eyes of mercy towards us, and after this, our exile, show on to us the blessed fruit of thy womb, Jesus. O clement, O loving, O sweet virgin Mary! Pray for us, O Holy Mother of God.

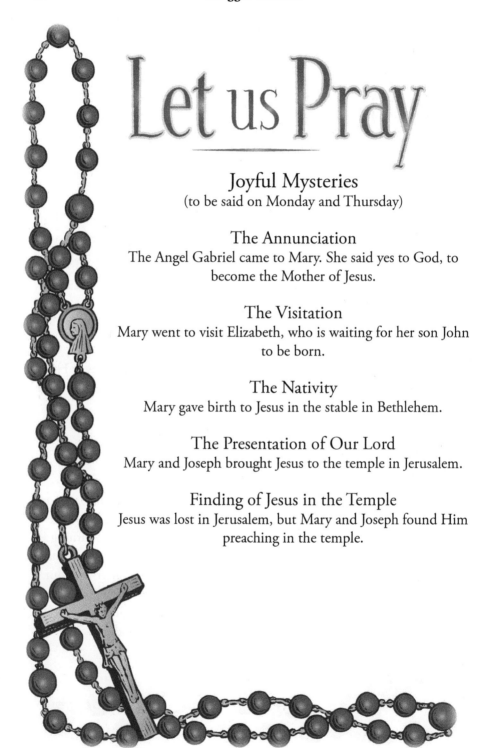

Let us Pray

Joyful Mysteries
(to be said on Monday and Thursday)

The Annunciation
The Angel Gabriel came to Mary. She said yes to God, to become the Mother of Jesus.

The Visitation
Mary went to visit Elizabeth, who is waiting for her son John to be born.

The Nativity
Mary gave birth to Jesus in the stable in Bethlehem.

The Presentation of Our Lord
Mary and Joseph brought Jesus to the temple in Jerusalem.

Finding of Jesus in the Temple
Jesus was lost in Jerusalem, but Mary and Joseph found Him preaching in the temple.

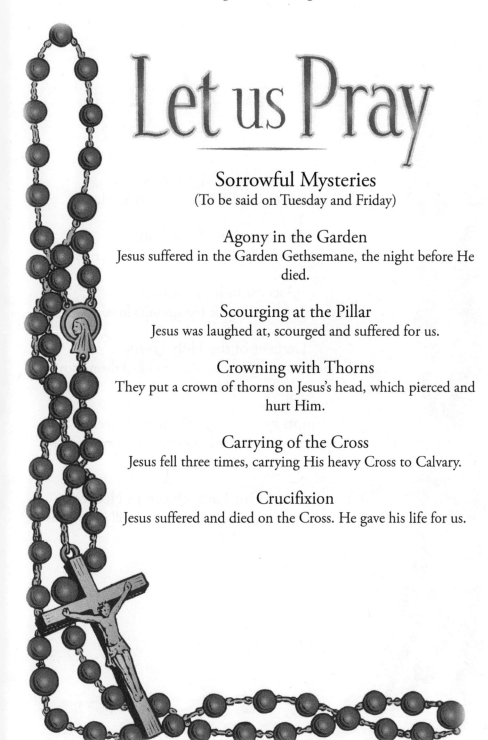

Let us Pray

Sorrowful Mysteries
(To be said on Tuesday and Friday)

Agony in the Garden
Jesus suffered in the Garden Gethsemane, the night before He died.

Scourging at the Pillar
Jesus was laughed at, scourged and suffered for us.

Crowning with Thorns
They put a crown of thorns on Jesus's head, which pierced and hurt Him.

Carrying of the Cross
Jesus fell three times, carrying His heavy Cross to Calvary.

Crucifixion
Jesus suffered and died on the Cross. He gave his life for us.

Let us Pray

Glorious Mysteries
(To be said Wednesday, Saturday, and Sunday)

Resurrection of our Lord
Jesus rose from the dead and appeared to His people.

Ascension into Heaven
Jesus went to Heaven while His Apostles looked on.

Descent of the Holy Spirit
The Holy Spirit came to His Apostles and filled them with joy and hope.

Assumption of Our Lady into Heaven
Our Lady was carried up to Heaven from where we are always in Her Care.

Coronation of Our Lady Queen of Heaven
Our Lady is crowned Queen of Heaven and will go to Jesus for us.

Who's to Blame?

The innocent who suffered, at the evil one's hand,
Will one day rejoice, In God's own land
Please turn back, before it's too late
Pray the Rosary together, to save our faith

Who's to blame for the Sin and the Shame?
That caused innocent children so much pain
It's time to make a stand, and protect our youth
For the sake of their suffering, we must prevail
And make those who hurt them, lift off their veil

Let's not forget, where there is goodness, there is evil too,
We cannot tarnish everyone, for things, they did not do
The TV and the media will have us believe we do
To sell an extra paper and make a buck or two
When Jesus picked the disciples, he picked Judas too
I wonder why? I leave that up to you.

Remember, there is good and bad in all of us, I'm sure you agree
But with prayer, love, and forgiveness, the goodness will shine through
Then justice will prevail and the Serpent will have no choice
But to return, to its fiery grave.

Now who's to blame I ask you, is it me or you?
Or is it the evil one, who's out to get us too!

The evil one is hard at work, to turn us all, against the Church
When God's Words to us, he did say, love my Son, for He will come,
Judgement Day
And all of us that destruction seek, will surely fall, at the Devil's feet
And Our Lady's tears would have fallen in vain, for her Son who died, in so
much pain, to save us all from the Devil's reign

I for one know who's to blame, for I know, what he's out to gain
He wants the power of God above, with help from the lost souls of this world
I will not follow the devil's route; I'll always follow the Holy Book
For it's there I know I found the Truth
So pray the Rosary and go to Church and put your trust in the Good Lord's Word
We cannot live our lives in hate, pain, and destruction, that's its trait
If we live our life through love, it will surely lead us to the Heavens above.
God's way alone is the safe path home.

Maggie Heston
March 2010

The words of this beautiful poem came to me one night after praying the
Rosary. I asked God to guide all the Clergy, our Holy Father the Pope, and
all the people involved in the Catholic Church. I also prayed for all the
innocent who suffered. Sometimes we are all too quick to judge people. The
evil one divides and concurs, and when we judge, that is how we help the
evil one to destroy everything in its track. Is it not in the Holy Bible 'judge
not and we shall not be judged'? God alone will pluck the weeds from the
vegetable plot. The only tools he needs are our prayers for all concerned.
God is also all forgiving and when we repent and put right what we have
done wrong and pray for those who are weaker, we slowly but surely push
the evil one away. Then and only then, the healing process begins.

The Rat Race

Maggie Heston
15 September 2010

Tears of blood, oh how they flow, from a mother's eyes who loves us so
For what she sees on God's earth is the reign of the devil devouring her flock
Every corner of the globe, so plain to be seen from the heavens above
War and destruction, hatred and pain
False prophets spreading lies and deceit through the human chain
Making promises of huge financial gain, for those who sign on the dotted line, selling their souls for an easier time
The few that are still spreading the good Lord's Word are belittled and trampled on, buried in the mud
Our Father in Heaven, o how He must hurt, for the women who sacrificed so very much, to save us all from the Devil's clutch
The ultimate sacrifice God and our Lady made for us, they watched Jesus being nailed to the Cross
They heard Their Son cry out in pain, begging His Father to please forgive them, for they know not what they do
The serpent has blinded all of them too
Let this be a lesson to the human race, stamp out the evil, follow God's saving grace
How many of you are suffering today with all the wealth that has come your way?
Look around, all you will see, broken families torn apart, everyone seems to have empty hearts
Our youth, are they all lost to us, alcohol, drugs, violence, sex, what follows this route sadly, destruction, death
Young lives wiped out far too soon
Why did we not teach them right from wrong?
Are we so lost in our own pain
We couldn't see, where we were leading them?
Pick up the rosary beads, start to pray
Teach your children, the good Lord's way
Place the sacred heart within your homes
The biggest battle all of us fight is the battle between wrong and right
Enough destruction we have seen
Please put your trust in our Heavenly Queen.

Quote: Contentment is not the fulfilment of your wish but the appreciation of what we have.

From the Womb to the Tomb

The piercing cry to his mother's ears, brings great joy and happy tears
As she lovingly cradles him in her arms, hoping and praying he'll come to no harm
She knows the long road he will travel alone, with signposts telling him which way to turn
And coloured lights flashing, saying go or stay but many of those signs have been turned the wrong way
Her duty to him is her true guiding hands and father's wisdom and support as he grows into a man
The time has now come for him to move on from the love and warmth of a family so strong
Finding his way through troubles and strife
Making decisions and hoping they're right
Falling by the wayside, sometimes he's led wrong, the lure of narcotics, wine, women, and song

As one day falls slowly into the next, slowly realising life is not a quick fix.
For the true way of life is reality to face the wise words of his parents and God's saving grace.
The future for him is now looking bright; his goal in life, is now in sight

The hurt he caused he is ready to heal
That's why he's now, making his appeal
If you stand up, for things you know are true, there's a better life out there
for you
Do not live your life in doom or gloom,
Live life to the full
From the womb to the tomb

Quote: Quick fixes are slow breakers, hope springs eternal.

Maggie Heston
6 October 2010

Mother Ireland

I can see a tear form in your eyes, Mother Ireland
Just like it was back then,
But this time it's not caused by the hand of a stranger,
But by the deeds of our governments.
Lies and deceit money and greed that's what brought Mother Ireland to its knees.
Stocks and shares, millionaires, nobody told us the banks were bare.
They ran with the hounds, ignoring the hares, they gambled and lost the gold in the pot,

And left Mother Ireland broke and distraught.
To the rest of the world we're the laughing stock,
Borrowing more money to fill the empty pot.
Greedy men with suits and pens, signatures, signatures is there no end.
Government officials, businessmen, free to do what suited them,
People not realising our heritage now at an end?
Did the famine not teach us anything?
Proud to be Irish it used to be fact
Our forefathers made sure of that
Cromwell, Ahern, and Kenny the weakest links
Mother Ireland now needs a complete change.
Brothers and sisters, please stand proud
Raise your voices, stroke your pens. Please help Mother Ireland smile again.
This applies not just to Ireland but to the whole world, what legacy are we
leaving our children?

Forty Shades of Green

Thatched houses, country lanes, brightly lit turf fires, smoke curling to the sky
Land of saints and scholars, that was our emerald isle.

The smell of freshly mown meadows, the sound of children at play, the
fishermen whistling loudly, as their boats come into the bay. A helping hand
to neighbours, that's how we passed our days.

Homemade bread and butter, fresh vegetables from the plot, cured salted
bacon from the barrel, a cup or two of buttermilk, fresh kally from the pot.
Six o'clock the angelus, followed by the rosary, the family prayed together,
content and so happy.

Folklore, songs and stories, the neighbours joined as well, tea and current
bread for the children, adults sipping the homemade brew, sometimes the
fun went on through the night, until the cock, he crew. Little money to be
had, big families to be reared. Hard work and strong belief always pulled
us through.
Reaching out to others, that's what us Irish do.

The Celtic tiger galloped in, sweeping our land with a grin.
Bigger houses to be built, fast cars, restaurant bills. Credit cards replaced the
cash, governments telling us it's going to last, supermarkets with posh names,
offering us big savings.
Both parents out at work, grannies and granddads forgot, they weren't quick
enough. Crèches replacing them you see, keeping up with the Joneses, the
thing to be, forgetting our neighbours, too busy to stop and chat.

The Celtic tiger galloped in, destroying our forty shades of green.
And our good friends and neighbours were nowhere to be seen. For forty
pieces of silver, our souls became unclean. Sunday mass a thing of the past,
traditional Ireland went out of the window so fast, family life alien to us,
Irish people now are so out of touch.
The rat race on for the sake of a buck, whatever happened to our Irish luck?
Technology taking over from the human brain, replacing our quick wit and
humour, turning us into modern machines.
All that left for us to do, is to turn back to God and His heavenly crew, that's
when we will find peace once more.
Re-educate our children of days of yore, then once again we'll be proud to be
Irish, proud to be free, in our beautiful isle of Inishfree.

Maggie Heston
25 December 2011

When we strive for power, greed slips in slowly and somehow we seem to
forget what really matters. It's the little things in life that makes us who we
are. And the people we surround ourselves with are whom we become.

Totally Free

Sometimes I wonder, when I get the final call,
Were the highs and lows, really worth it all?
Because the highs I was on were really the lows,
And the lows were the ones that actually
fed my soul.

Now I realise the hard road in life was the one for me,
And the truth in life is what gives you the key.
The secret, be told, is reality you see.
The long way around is the quickest for me.

The voice in my heart was not reaching me,
My head begs to differ, that's what's bothering me.

If the definition of both of them, I could find,
The blinkers off, I'd no longer be blind.
The advice of others, I used to believe,
But I've thrown that aside, I'm now listening to me.

Now the road may be full of troubles and strife,
But from now on, I'm taking back, my own life!
The skeleton is now buried, that belonged to me.
The burden now dealt with,
I'm totally free.

Maggie Heston
27 July 2007

Making a life-changing decision may seem hard at the time. Taking one step at a time, believing in oneself, throwing the fear away, and never to be afraid of the unknown.

Our Lady of Medugorje

Oh lovely Lady dressed in blue, where would my life be without you?
Thank you for caring so much for me. When I was lost and could not see,
You took my heart and set me free, now no longer lost or all alone.
You introduced me to your Son, And He in turn, just like you
Guided me on the road of prayer and truth. Lovely Lady dressed in blue,
Your messages I'll help pass on for you, That God Our Lord up above, is
trying to save the lost souls of this world.

My Lady thank you for not giving up on me, when I was weak and fell down
at your feet,
You took my hand and kissed my cheek, and said to me, 'Do not be weak,
when you suffer, others heal.'
And as the tears rolled down my face, I felt the comfort of your loving embrace.

You took my hand and whispered your special plan for me,
'Medugorje is calling out your name,
Put your trust in me, lost souls will gain many favours through my Holy name.
And gain the Grace of God through His special plan.
You guided me to this beautiful place, so I too, could feel his saving grace,
Thank you, my Lady, for leading me, on the journey of God, Jesus, and Thee.

The rat race of man is not for me, false prophets promising the golden key,
Striving for wealth that is not real, fooling mankind with false pretence,
All of this flowing from the dark, dark prince.

If we follow her plan, we all will see, the meaning of Our Lady of Medugorje,
In this special place we will quickly find, moving from the darkness into the light,
Messages Our Lady passed to the seven children are true.
Thousands of people from all walks of life,
The Medugorje experience, they will carry for life.
Passing on the message to those who will listen.
In this beautiful valley, it's plain to be seen, renewal of souls, through Our
Heavenly Queen,
Carrying graces home, to family and friends, Their spiritual journey about to
begin.

Oh lovely Lady dressed in blue, you held my hand and helped me through,
And when I fail, as I sometimes do, I know that I can always rely on you,
To make me strong and carry me through.

To overcome our burdens and set us free, you said to pray the Rosary,
And while in prayer, the more we understand, the importance of reaching out hands,
To family, friends, neighbours, and strangers too,
One good deed a day may well do. The crosses they carry made lighter by you.

So lovely Lady dressed on blue, my life's journey, is to follow you,
And while I'm praying, the more I understand, why you reached out and took my hand, then led me to a foreign land, The gift you gave, is not mine you see,
It's to guide others, so they too can be free,
In this special place called Medugorje.

And to all the pilgrims who visit this special place, Find for yourself, your own space, whether it be on the mountain side,
Or Saint James's Church, where Our Lady's Son can be found.
Close your eyes, place your trust in God, Problems then, you will no longer have. Then turn to the beautiful Lady dressed in blue,
And thank her from your heart, for leading you.

Maggie Heston
12 July 2011

As He Sleeps

I watch him as he sleeps, wondering what happened to the years.
I remember the words said when he first popped into this world.
His heart is weak, fever high, if not put into special care, he'll surely die.
I fought the tears as he was admitted to ICU,
Praying to our Lady, please don't take him too.
I know that night my prayers were heard, next morning the doctors said he
was starting to fight.
From that day on he fought so strong, hospital appointments went on and on.
You never complained, took it all in your stride,
I was so proud of how hard you tried.
Although a lot of time you were in pain,
It did not stop you joining in the fun and the games.
Education at the start was tough, but with a little help, you strut your stuff.
Sixteen years you may well be, six foot tall as handsome can be.
The girls queue up to catch your smile, all your friends take up your time.
But as busy as your life may be, you always have a hug and kiss for me.
Proudest mother in the world, that's me.
Watching you sleep, content as can be,
Just beside you on the window sill, a statue of Our Lady of Medugorje.
And at her feet a candle lights, put there by you before you said goodnight.
You often asked when you were young, why God and Our Lady took your
twin sister home,
This is what I said to you, God and Our Lady wanted an Angel too.
(Dedicated to my son Patrick—your strength, courage, and faith is an
inspiration to us all. Where Science Ends, God Begins, May Our Holy
Mother always be your guide.)

Maggie Heston
18 December 2010

My Boys

Eighteen months between the two, they always stuck together like glue,
The rough and the tumble when they were small nearly drove me up the wall.
Into the teenager years with a bang, falling out, making up, hanging out together, and acting tough.
Telltales on each other, they never would do, saying, 'Mum, don't ask us, 'cos that's not cool.'
As the years pass, directions for them change: parties, girlfriends, work, emigration. One settled down at home, the other decided to travel alone, missing each other they do not say, but the bond that they share, no one can break, they might as well have been twins, they are so alike, yet so different, but the minute they came into my life, I knew they were special, they are my boys.

Maggie Heston
13 December 2010

(Dedicated to my sons Michael and Denis. Thank you for all the joy, love, and happiness you have given me and your dad over the years. May God, our Lady and the holy saints and angels guide ye always!)
(Children are truly a gift from God.)

A Message to Mummy

Please, Mummy, don't be sad, I would have stayed if I could.
But God decided the Time was not right.
I'm sorry I left in the night, left you and Dad sad and empty inside.
I know you cried in disbelief, it makes me sad to see you grieve.
I know right now it's hard for you to understand, but one day, Mummy, I'll grasp your hand, I'll fill yours and Daddy's hearts with pure sweet love and we will bond together just like a glove.
When God decides the Time Is Right, he will let me back into your life.
I promise you, Mummy, I'll make you smile.
Just wait for me, a little while.
For, Mummy, all us Angels that's been and gone,
Never stay away too long, we always return to where we belong.

Maggie Heston
December 2010

(Dedicated to my little angel who fought so hard to come into this world. God and Our Lady decided they wanted an Angel too. When I look into your twin brother's eyes, I'm always reminded of you. XXX)

Blessed Mother Teresa's Prayer

People are often unreasonable, irrational, and self-centred,
Forgive them anyway,
If you are kind, people may accuse you of selfish, ulterior motives,
Be kind anyway,
If you are successful, you will win some unfaithful friends and some genuine enemies,
Succeed anyway
What you spend years creating, others could destroy overnight,
Create anyway
If you find serenity and happiness, some may be jealous,
Be happy anyway
The good you do today, will often be forgotten,
Do good anyway
Give the best you have, and it will never be enough,
Give your best anyway,

In the final analysis, it is between you and God,
It was never between you and them anyway.

Mother Teresa devoted her life to helping people, especially the poor. She will be remembered by many generations to come. She moved mountains and never let anybody stand in her way. May all those good people that carry on her good work be guided by God!

Day by Day

You must come to me little children,
Simple and pure of heart
Trust is the foundation
Of a loving and peaceful heart.
If you are weary,
Lonesome or sad
Lean on Me, pray My name, call My Son, through the rosary of liberation.
He will enfold you, His heart will open to you.
So my children, do not fear, for your Father is always near.
Holy is the name, the Father the Son and the Holy Spirit.
Turn to me, your Mother, and I will always be there, to pass on your prayers.
Then as My graces fill your soul, and you are made whole.
Fears will disappear, because you will know that God is taken you in hold
and now walks with you.
Day by Day by Day.

26 January 2010

The Rosary of Liberation

The Rosary of Liberation begins with the Apostles' Creed and ends with the Hail Holy Queen. In place of the Our Father on the large beads, we will pray the Words, if the Son makes you free you will be free indeed.
In the place of the Hail Mary, on the small beads pray Jesus have mercy on me, Jesus Heal me, Jesus save me, and Jesus free me.
If you are praying for your family or friends, you will pray, if Jesus makes my family, friends free, they will be free indeed.
When you start to pray this Rosary, you will feel its power. It's also very important to pray the Holy Rosary. The family that prays together stays together. Please pass on to family and friends. I will be forever grateful to the family who passed on this Rosary to me.

ℐ Prayer to the ℋoly ℐngels

I/We ask through the divine intervention of our Lord Jesus Christ, Our Lady, and all the Holy saints and Holy Angels,

For the Holy Spirit to descend upon me/us,

I/We ask the Archangel Michael surround us with his protective wings and ward off all evil.

I/We ask the Holy Angels of Healing, the Holy Angels of Direction, The Holy Angels of Wisdom, The Holy Angels of Protection, the Holy Angels of Knowledge, the Holy Angels of Guidance, the Holy Angels of Harmony, the Holy Angels of Understanding, the Holy Angels of serenity, the Holy Angels of Peace, the Holy Angels of Love, The Holy Angels of Faith, the Holy Angels of Finance, etc.

I/We ask this through the Divine Intervention or Our Lord Jesus Christ, Our Lady and all the Holy Saints and Holy Angels.

Amen

One Our Father,
Three Hail Mary's,
The Guardian Angel Prayer.
This Prayer came to Maggie when she was a child, and she has believed in its power ever since.

Maggie Heston
02 April 2012

Always remember, in our darkest moments we are never alone. There are thousands of Holy Angels unemployed, why? We forget to ask for their help.

The Little Cottage

Where the mountains or Mourne sweep down to the sea
Stands a little cottage sheltered by trees bought for investment, rented out
for a while; to live there, no, not his style.
Little did he realise, one day things would change, finding himself alone sad
and deranged.
Life torn apart, tough decisions to make, falling deeper in debt, wondering
which road to take.
Taken time out to find world, realising the cottage would shelter him.
As night turned to day and day turned to night, conclusion he came to, he
never lived his own life.
A long time ago, throwing his free will aside, and like lots of others got lost
in the tide.
Married before he became a man, there never was a proper plan.
Of to the city he decided to go, making lots of money putting on a show.
Fat wallet, fast life, socialising every night.
Music and laughter, whisky and gin, loose women, opportunities to sin, this
way of life wasn't really him.
How could he fill the empty space within?

Then a beautiful Lady came into his life and gently brought him to a place
so Holy and bright.
Thus helped him open his eyes to the true path in life.
She whispered softly in his prayers one night saying, 'Please listen to me.
You must write you must write.'
She promised to help and guide him along.
She gave him the words of such beautiful songs.
One of them being, a little piece of Heaven the meaning of Medugorje and
the messages of our Heavenly Queen.
Why am I telling this story to you, read on if you want to know.
In that little cottage overlooking the sea, that same man sits there judged by
others, not me,
For I too, like him, was empty inside, searching and searching following the
tide and that same beautiful Lady also carried me along, to write beautiful
poetry and help pass her messages on.
And guiding two sad hearts until they became one.
I may be judged by others too, but I'll keep following Our Lady my whole
life through.

Maggie Heston
15 December 2009

God never intervenes with our free will. No matter where life takes us, we
are all on a journey. Sometimes it is hard to understand, even harder for
others, when we branch out in different directions. How do our forests grow
and branch out? Does the wind not change direction? How beautiful would
our forests be if man did not intervene?

Our Lady's Tears (Medugorje)

Looking at the statue on the Holy mountain side.
I watch the tears flow freely from our Holy Mother's eyes.
The heartbreak that she feels is not for herself, but for the way us humans
choose to lead our lives.
She pities the old woman kneeling at her feet praying for her daughter who
works on the dark and dreary streets.
She pities the old man sitting on the rock, hands covering his face, grieving
for his only grandson, found hanging in the loft.
She pities the young mother who cradles her baby on her lap, praying her
estranged husband will find his own way back.
She pities the pilgrims who kneel in front of her each day, forgetting their
own troubles, for their loved ones they come to pray.
She pities the lost souls of this world, why did they not listen to her beloved
Son's Words.
She pities the drug dealers for their souls are black with sin from dragging
her innocent children straight to the devil's den.

The pity she feels for the pilgrims on this Holy Mountain does not go on
unseen for many, many graces are granted to all of them.
She pities those looking for a quick fix on the street, if only they could join
the pilgrims who are praying at her feet.
She knows if the whole world could join together in prayer just once a day,
then God would be free to make our world a better place.
Then there would be no more weeping statues, no hatred, wars, or pain, no
more tsunamis, earthquakes, floods or storms.
No more blaming God for the evil on this earth and no more people
knocking God's Holy Church.
So next time you meet a pilgrim on their return from a Holy place, take time
to listen to them, it could be your saving grace.
The pity I feel on this Holy Mountain today it's not for mankind but for our
Holy Mother's tear-stained face.
And the messages she has given to this world for the Salvation of our souls is
all too often ignored for the darkness we have chosen.
So anyone who reads this, please read it once again and remember the
sacrifice Our Holy Mother made way back then.
So let us join together and bow our heads in prayer, and ask God's
forgiveness for the weakness we all share.
When we meet our maker, and this we will for sure, the truth will come out
about the evil one who lures.

Maggie Heston
27 June 2013

This poem is very close to my heart inspired by the many years I have
travelled on pilgrimage to Medugorje. In this beautiful valley, I really
found our Lady, and in finding her, I found myself. The seven visionaries
have passed on messages given to them by our Lady to the world. I wonder
how many are listening: peace, peace, and only peace together with prayer,
reaching out to others, loving each other, Our Lady does not ask for much.
Medugorje has given me so much, including peace of mind. Anybody who
has travelled there will always go back. It's a little piece of Heaven.

The Voice Within

If I were to get a chance again,
I know I'd follow the voice within.
For too many times I have to say I was blind, and followed other people's ways.
But if I knew then, what I know now, I'd believe in myself and ignore the crowd.
What I have learned over the years, from the ups and the downs, the joys and the fears, all the while searching in life for what could be found inside myself.
But now I'm old, feeble and grey, and coming to the end of my day. Advice to others if I may give, hold a pen on your fingertip, write down what you are searching for, address the letter to your good God,
Wrap it up in an envelope of gold,
Post it directly to your own soul.

If we listen to our gut feeling, we will never take the wrong path.

Maggie Ahern
02 April 2012

My Father, My Friend

I will not remember you, with sadness nor with tears
I'll remember all the good times, your advice, your wisdom
Shared laughter, love and tears
I'll remember the conversations late into the night
The songs you sang, the music you played
I'll remember with happiness.
Your precious smiling face, I will never forget.
I still picture you sitting, on your fireside chair
A warm welcome for everyone, that's the way you were
And when my road gets rough and rocky,
I know you still give me a helping hand from the heavens above
I sometimes feel you by my side, just an inch too short to touch
A father's love a blessing, and no, it doesn't die with death
The day you went to heaven, you left your love with me, here on Earth
You weren't just my Father; you were my best friend too
May you rest in peace, Daddy, until we meet again,
Please put your arms around him God and kiss his smiling face,
For he is so, so special and can never be replaced.

Maggie Heston
4 December 2010

Daddy, if I could just have one hour with you again, it would be worth my weight in gold. When God took you home, it broke my heart. Going through that grief brought me to a greater understanding of life and what matters to me. Your journey in life at times was not easy. You gave so much and took so little. I, like my mother, and brothers, sisters, grandchildren, great-grandchildren, and all those who loved you will always carry you in our hearts. One of your favourite sayings has been 'Life is to be cherished. Smother your children with love.' Daddy, I wonder what you think today when you see what's happening in our country and indeed the world. Pray to God that the little children will be given a chance. Another one of your quotes has been 'When a daisy seed is planted and tended to with love and care, one day it will grow into a beautiful flower.'

Maggie Heston

Vision Through the Window

The old lady stooped low to the fire; she raked the few remaining coals together and placed some small dry sticks carefully on to the sparks. She watched patiently as the first flames began to lick hungrily at the fresh morsels of timber, the flames rose bright and merrily as the draught from the chimney drew new life into its heart. The old woman sighed contently, and she watched from her knees, the result of her labour come to fruition, then she reached over to the turf box and proceeded to stack each sod carefully around the flames, and in time, she knew this action would bring on a more enduring heat. She slowly picked herself up and shuffled over to her armchair. She eased herself into the chair and reached over to the table to pick up her rosary beads and laid them gently on her lap; her eyes turned slowly towards the fireplace and fixed upon the randomly flickering and dancing tongues of fire. Their hypnotic motions and forms eased her mind and body from the fears and loneliness of the day, and its heat penetrated her thin robe like a balm to her cold and thin old skin.

Her eyes danced from this point to that in the fire, from this strong flame slowly receding, to that one just growing to fruition. Her eyes followed this dance of life and death gleefully, its crackling cries echoing through her soul, to find a mirror of itself in her own life, waiting there to greet it.

It was a joyous meeting, etched deep like a melody, as only the great passage of life can bring.

Jubilation so great, that it touched a core of deep grief, reminding herself that she could not experience this feeling forever. It was a moment in time, which maybe gladly, maybe sadly, comes but occasionally. As she stared, her mind wandered from the manic immediacy of the fire, and brought her to other places in her mind, far removed from the here and now. She recalled the love of her life, her husband and lifelong partner, she remembered their first kiss, how their eyes locked as they prayed their marriage vows together. The delights of their love, forever embedded in their hearts, but brightly still shone the love in her eyes as onwards she remembers many happy days, months, years, through the joys of first greeting her children into the world and staring with deep love and devotion at the man who gave her such beautiful and precious gifts.

Eleven times they had been blessed, and only once they had been cursed, onwards her mind sped to the joys of seeing the world made new, once again, through the eyes of their children. Their first stumbling steps, their inevitable falls, their trials and tribulations had never failed to lift her heart when heavy and careworn. She was always reminded at those times, that as we are to them, so are they to others, and her own troubles, like her children's, never lingered.

Her mind wandered only briefly, at the sad departure of her children, preferring to remember them as they were in their early youth, rather than the time they had to leave to seek their own lives and challenges. She recalls the many letters filling her with joyous relief with news of their progress in foreign lands and on their many return visits where her family were united together again around the homestead fireplace. She remembered the love and contentment she shared with the man that gave her so much. Her memory froze in time, to hold the gaze once more and for the last time to feel his hand grasp hers before he slowly let go and slipped away from her, with the realisation that there remains a void in her life that would never again be filled.

Now back in the present, the fresh pain brought tears to her eyes, her heart so heavy with longing; she swallowed the familiar lump in her throat and blinked to clear her eyes. She found herself staring into the embers of the fire once again burnt low, leaving the cold to pluck at her weary body; she wondered to herself whether she should start the fire once again or would she just allow the cold to finally fall over the old homestead and give in to this longing to be back in his arms once again. She slowly picks up her rosary beads and begins to pray the rosary, leaving the decision in his hands, trusting in God's plan.

Maggie Heston

27 August 2009

This short story is about my mother Bridget Heston, whom I idolise. She married my father James when she was just eighteen years old. She went on to have eleven children. All her life she has cared for her family and extended family members. Her home is full of love. There will always be a hot dinner and a warm bed for those who visit. And they are from all corners of the world. She and my father passed on to us and our children their deep love of God and respect for others. I was inspired to write Vision through the Window shortly after my father passed on (RIP). On visiting her one day I watched her through the window preparing for the day. To lose someone close to us is heartbreaking, especially a lifelong partner. There's a gap left that no one can fill, not even loving children. My mother's greatest comfort is in knowing that my dad, her husband, is with God and is watching over us all.

Listen to My Whispers

Be still, and listen to my whispers
For I am reaching out for you

When sorrow surround you and dark clouds descend
And you think you're not able to go on, to the end
Just look at the light I am shining on you
And take my hand, and we'll both see it through

I stood with my son, at the foot of the cross
Till the last drop of blood, from his body was lost
And I'll stand with you too, when you call out my name
I'll give you comfort and ease all your pain

So keep talking with me, just as much as you can
And I will always reach out for your hand
I will guide and protect you wherever you may be
For your life will be sweeter with my rosary

Wording: this beautiful poem was given to Maggie Heston and Gerry
Flanagan.
Gerry Flanagan, singer and song writer, recorded Mother's Whispers in
Many different languages.
And it is only one of many given to Gerry by our Lady.
If you would like to hear more of his inspirational work,
Visit: WWW.GerryFlanagan.org
Or email: Gmmpfla1@yahoo.co.uk

Maggie Heston
August 2008

Honor's Star

There is a new star shining brightly way up in the sky
It first appeared on Monday as Honor closed her eyes
When the angels came to take her, to her heavenly home
They left the star to thank all of you who mourn
For the love, care, and friendship to Honor, you have shown
To her loving family, please do not be sad
For she knew it was time to visit Mom, Dad, and Pat
Mary, Breege, Clare, and Tom, she thanks sincerely
From the bottom of her heart, for all the love and kindness
Shown from you and your families, while she was here on earth
The special way you loved her, she will not forget
She leaves you all with a loving kiss
Goodbye, God bless.

Children and adults with special needs truly are a gift from God. Spending time in their company lifts our hearts; their love is unconditional and they trust everyone. They never judge; we can all take a leaf out of their book.

Maggie Heston
2 November 2010

Labour of Love

Before you grow old
Remember my words
Learning is better than silver and gold
For silver and gold will soon fade away
But learning and virtue will never decay.

These words I remember my father reciting to me
When I was a child
In later years I passed same on to my children.
I thank my great-grandmother Kit Reilly
For it was she who passed them on to my father
James Heston.
May they both rest in peace!

25 June 2013

Three Miles of Country Road

It looked happy when I was happy; when I was sad it looked sad too
And if I was feeling lonely, it sure looked lonely too
For it's been with me since I was born, and it will be there when I go
I took my first steps on life's journey, on those three miles of country road

When I'm far away from home, my thoughts go back in time
To the hedgerows and the sycamore, and the ones I left behind
Far away fields look green, they say, but I can tell you no
I'd sooner have stayed and made my way, on those three miles of country road

The first day that I walked to school, in the grasp of my father's hand
My mother waving from the door, sure her poor heart ached that morn
And when the time it came around, for me to cross the foam
I had to part with a heavy heart, from the three miles of country road

The day my father passed away, there was a tear in every eye
The hawthorn seemed to bow their heads, and the bluebell seemed to cry
We walked so slowly to the little church; I just didn't want to let him go
But it seemed to say, it'll be OK, those three miles of country road

If only I could walk again, that three-mile stretch
And put my hand into the hand that walked with me, back then.
For he was my idol, my best friend, he taught me everything I know
His words of wisdom I won't forget, on those three miles of country road

Any man can be a father; it takes a special father to also be a friend.

Maggie Heston
August 2008

You Got Me!

Maggie Heston
20 September 2009

You got me the moment I first heard your voice

You got me the moment I turned and looked into your eyes

You got me the moment I responded to your smile

You got me back then and I did not realise

You got me the moment our friendship began

You walked with me, talked with me, then held my hand

You got me the moment I first sat by your side and shouldered your troubles
while your voice sang out

You got me the moment you first hugged me tight, and when your lips
touched my lips, it just felt so right

You got me the moment our bodies entwined, so much love and emotion
flowing from you and bonding with mine

You got me, my darling, and now you are mine.

(Dedicated to my mother and father)

Twin Flames

Maggie Heston
April 2010

Our lives started out in much the same way, born with the connection
But journeying in two different ways
Then fate stepped in and showed us the way, brought us together, the
connection was made
Two hearts beat as one, the feeling so strong
We did not set out to hurt anyone
We couldn't extinguish this eternal flame

The flames keep burning, ever so bright, we cannot run away, we cannot hide
The feelings that were buried for most of our lives, came to the surface and
reached for the light
Bonding two souls that were meant to be, now journeying together for all
eternity

So all of you that are still out there, looking for love and someone to care
Take your time, please be aware
What guided us will guide you too, to where that flame is burning for you
And when those flames join together
This is the love that will last forever.

My Twin Flame

The very first day you walked into my life
Everything left me, the troubles and strife
For the empty space I was looking to fill, is now as complete as it ever will
But when the miles separate us, and we are apart
I'm not complete because you have my heart
When I'm lonely on those cold winter nights, I would give all I own to be holding you tight.
But one day I know it will be worth all the pain, for our lives will be complete when we are together forever, my twin flame.

Maggie Heston
21 August 2010

Jackie

I've known Jackie many years, together we share life's joys and life's fears.
Muddling along together, one as mad as the other.
She is always willing to lend a helping hand, a kinder heart you wouldn't find in this land.
A smile for a stranger, advise for the young, helping anyone that comes along.
The times I share with her are precious to me, 'cause there's always a laugh with Jackie you see.
Like the day Bridget asked us to whitewash the shed, Jackie grabbed the paintbrush and nodded her head.
Bridget gave the orders, as the job Jackie led.
Half way through admiring her work, Jackie asked Bridget what she taught,
Proper leaches Bridget said, 'The job I could do much better myself.
For it's not on my whitewash your minds are at all, but over beyond in the local bar.'
Jackie said with a glint in her eye, 'You're right, Bridget, I'm off for a while.'
So off she went, with myself in tow.
Two hours later, brush in hand, I've never seen as much whitewash in the land.
When Bridget went back to the shed, for her cows to be fed, sure the poor old woman nearly died with shock, there was no trace of her flock.
Only snow white walls and a note from Jackie, saying I finished the job.
Bridget was about to walk away, when a moo moo from the corner it did stray.
'The bloody egits,' said Bridget out loud, 'they have only whitewashed all of me cows.
And not a bit of dinner I'll give them today, they better run fast and stay out of me way.'
(Dedicated to my best friend Jackie Kennedy. I will always cherish our friendship. And from Jackie and me, Bridget, you're a legend.)

Footprints in the Snow

Silently it falls to earth
White flakes, cold, but soft to touch
Blanketing the ground, so angelic to look at.
Holding hands the couple passed me by
Their love as pure as the clear blue sky
Their footprints they leave side by side
They're so engrossed in each other.
What a beautiful sight!
With the snow, their footprints will fade away
But I pray to God, their love it will stay.

Maggie Heston
25 October 2010

(In memory of my wonderful time spent, Tyrol, Austria, 2010)

A Change of Heart

A young man sat in a lonely, cold, old room.
Sweat dripping from his body, fearful of the unknown.
A rope lay dangling beside him, he praying to God as a last request
The strength to pick up the rope and put the noose around his neck.

His life three years ago, so different.
A family, a career, and a nice home, until the curse of narcotics took over, destroying all that he owned.
Now, a shell of the man he once was.
In his head so much frustration, wondering what went wrong.

For so long nothing else bothered him, only when and where he could get his next quick fix from.
The people he loves dearly flashing through his muddled head, believing their lives would be easier if only he were dead.
But a change of heart came quickly, when he was distracted by his phone, for his Guardian Angel came to his rescue in the form of his young son.

'Daddy, I miss and love you, won't you please, please come home?
I'll show you my football card collection.
Oh, Daddy, we'll have so much fun.'

And as his son was talking, the tears rolled down his face.
A promise to his son he made.
'I'll pick you up in the morning, and this time I won't be late.'
For the first time in three years, he really prayed to God, thanking him from deep within his heart for the phone call he just had.
A second chance in life, this time he knew for the sake of his little son, his word he must carry through.
And by taking one day at a time, the man that was lost will once again be found.
Message to be read one day by my son

One day, Son, if you read this, and I pray to God you do.
The hurt I caused to you and others, I hope I can undo.
As you get older, you'll find out life is sometimes cruel, but there will always be someone there for you.
Dear Son, I thank God that I had you.

At our lowest, our holy guardian Angels work so hard to reach us. There is no such thing as coincidence, everything happens for a reason. God is always knocking open the door and let him in.

By Maggie Heston
19 March 2012

Hello, My Name Is Drugs

I destroy homes, tear families apart, take your children, and that's just the start. I'm more costly than diamonds, more costly than gold, the sorrow I bring is a sight to behold. And if you need me, remember I'm easily found. I live all around you, in schools and in town. I live with the rich, I live with the poor, I live down the street, and maybe next door. My power is awesome; try me, you'll see. But if you do, you may *never* break free. Just try me once and I might let you go, but try me twice, and I'll own your soul. When I possess you, you'll steal and you'll lie. You do what you have to just to get high. The crimes you'll commit, for my narcotic charms will be worth the pleasure you'll feel in my arms. You'll lie to your mother; you'll steal from your dad. When you see their tears, you should feel sad. But you'll forget your morals and how you were raised, I'll be your conscience, I'll teach you my ways. I take kids from parents, and parents from kids, I turn people from God, and separate friends. I'll take everything from you, your look and your pride; I'll be with you always, right by your side. You'll give up everything: your family, your home, your friends, your money, and then you'll be alone. I'll take and take, till you have nothing more to give. When I'm finished with you, you'll be lucky to live. If you try me, be warned this is no game. If given the chance, I'll drive you insane. I'll ravish your body; I'll control your mind. I'll own you completely; your soul will be mine. The nightmares I'll give you while lying in bed, the voices you'll hear from inside your head. The sweats, the shakes, the visions you'll see; I want you to know, these are all gifts from me. But then it's too late, and you'll know in your heart, that you are mine, and we shall not part. You'll regret that you tried me, they always so, but you came to me, not I to you. You knew this would happen. Many times you were told, but you challenged my power, and chose to be bold. You could have said no, and just walked away. If you could live that day over, now what would say? I'll be your master, you will be my slave; I'll even go with you when you go to your grave. Now that you have met me, what will you do? Will you try me or not? It's all up to you. I can bring you more misery than words can tell.

Come take my hand,

LET ME LEAD YOU TO HELL!

(To the unknown author that wrote this poem, wherever you may be, I'm sure you will not mind me sharing this beautiful piece of poetry to the world. It was written from the heart and please God will deter anybody else going down this road. May the Holy Angels protect and guide you as I am sure they already are.)

Hold On

When you're in despair
And you think there's no one who cares,

Remember the one who gave you life
And protected you through the night.

Till the darkest hour did pass, like the troubled mind
Sure it never last.

And with the rising of the sun, comes the love and warmth of nature's Mum.

Just hold on another while

She's on her way to make you smile.

Maggie Heston
20 July 2010

Another Fall

Why does it always happen to me?
This one's different, I led myself believe.
Deeper and deeper, my feelings went,
Loving him completely, blinded within.

Sharing our love, laughter and tears,
Helping each other with life's challenging fears.
Unbreakable the bond, is what I told my friends,
Confidential with life, total belief in him.

Slowly, but surely, the cracks began to show,
Arguments, hurtful words, the tears, they did flow,
Wondering why he distracted me so.
Disagreements, letting him win,
Thinking our relationship would find peace again.
Niggling doubts creeping in, the truth be told,
The signs there to be seen.
Finally, getting the wake-up call,
Picking myself up from another fall,
Another bad experience, thank God, that's all.

Maggie Heston
27 July 2012

Only when we forgive those who hurt us, we can move on and learn to love again.

After All Those Years

He never listened, too busy you see remote control, a glass of whiskey, backing the horses, grey hound track, fast cars.

Fast bucks, thinking he would never run out of luck. Waking up not able to move, Ambulance arrive, he's frightened and confused.

Two long weeks in the hospital bed, diagnoses, prognoses, the news not good.

Coming home to an empty flat, his mind racing like the grey hound track, dialling the number he calls for help.

Please, Mary, will you come, I just can't cope. A smiling face came through the door, years of hurt forgotten, the love still there, needing each other after all these years.

The sacred heart on the wall is bright again, shining with love.

The moral of the story, the news is good, don't live in regrets, it does us no good.

The best way to spend our days is with those we love and God's saving grace.

Dealing with the past always opens doors to the future, remember those we cared for and those who cared for us will always be there when we need them most. One smile is worth a thousand tears.

Wild Flowers

If all the wild flowers in the world today were plucked by you as a token of
love for me.
I have to say I'd be impressed, but my heart would hurt for the flower beds.
For flowers are there to please the eye, but not from a vase because they
wither and die.
Left grown in there flower bed, they flourish and bloom when properly fed.
Like the love you and I share, it blossomed from the root that was planted
with care.
For true love is like the beautiful wild flower, it always blooms year after year.
And when embraced by the healing rays of the sun.
Two hearts that's true will become as one

Maggie Heston
28 February 2012

A wild rose is the symbol of love, but must be handled with care. The petals
are soft to touch, and the stem is crowned with thorns. Love also must be
cherished and nurtured; if smothered, it will surly die.

Battle with the Bottle

I thought of you this morning, my heart was sad and low
As the coffin passed down the aisle, what a way to go
A man who gave into booze, the battle, he did lose
His life journey at an end, tomorrow forgotten, like he'd never been
But you are still living; you have so much to give
Please stop drowning your sorrows, live your life at will
Make up with your family; grab happiness with your sweetheart
The day you met her is the day you were blessed
For she is willing to fill the emptiness, that the alcohol has left
Take advice from me, Son, it's only for the best, for I know you better
Than you know yourself
This demon, you can overcome

Addiction is just a mask that shields us from the world. Behind every mask, there is a heart that hurts. Sometimes we have to try all the keys on the lock, the one that opens the door is always hidden amongst them, never give up trying.

Maggie Heston
4 December 2010

A Problem Aired

Is nobody listening?
Can anyone help?
Did we not hear their cries?
Why did they not know which way to go?
Why were they full of sorrow and woe?
Couldn't we tell they were at a crossroads?
Deeper and deeper their hearts sank
Eventually pushing them to the brink!

Why did they not stop for a moment and think?
There is always someone willing to listen
A parent, a teacher, maybe a friend
Even a stranger, perhaps a sibling

It may take a while to sort it out
Problems, like puzzles are always solved
Remember those people that ended their lives
Let their memories not fade but be a reminder to us
Life is precious, no problem too much
What bothers us deep inside is best shared and worked out
We cannot be helped
If we don't speak out!
A problem aired is a problem shared

Maggie Heston
30 November 2010

All we need is one person in life to believe in us. One person to listen and,
above all, one person whom we can trust.

I'm Old (Whatever)

Maggie Heston
24 November 2010

He said I'm getting old, there's nothing further from the truth.
I'm hanging on to my youth and giving him the bloody boot.
I may have wrinkles on my face, lumps and bumps about the place
Aches and pains, twisted veins, fag-stained teeth and chilblains.
When I talk, I start to wheeze, when I walk, it hurts my knees.
He says, 'Please, darling, slow down, or you'll surely end up in the ground.
Old age is upon us,' his favourite quote.
But sometimes I wonder as we get into bed with his ears in the drawer.
His teeth in a cup, one eye looking down from the wardrobe top.
His pyjamas buttoned to the top, he's off to sleep, what the heck!
While I'm left wondering what else, he's left on the shelf.
It surely can't be, it is, it's myself.
I really don't mind, I think with a grin, sure he's far too old to pull the women.
The boot I don't think I'll give to him, sure all he's got left is me and my owl bottle of Gin.
Sure I still got the eyesight, can wink at the men, whatever I do I'm not giving in.
And I'm as healthy now as I've ever been and ask for him his way of thinking is killing him.
Before I drop off for the night, I'll have an owl tipple o and pass me a light.

The wise man can act the fool, but the fool can't act the wise man.

Who Was with Me?

Maggie Heston
March 2010

Who was with me way back then when my life's journey was about to begin
Who laid me in my Mother's arms and protected me from all life's harms
Who guided me on to my little feet and held me up because they were still weak
Who healed my bruises when I did fall and gave me the strength to reach
my goals?
Who supported me all through school and even hung around when I acted
the fool

Who was with me, that sad, sad day when darkness descended and he
had his way
While he got up and walked away, the hurt and the sin it did stay
Who held me together through my teenage years and helped me live life
through the joys and the fears

Who came with me when I left home and travelled with me through foreign
lands?
Who was still with me when my children were born, helped teach them right
from wrong, who then took me in hand and led us back home to Ireland
Who knew when I was ready to cope, when the healing began and the
darkness eloped

Who was still with me when my work began and the sick children all
reached out their frail little hands
Who sent me those helpers who worked so hard, to ensure those children's
needs were catered for?

Who took me back down memory lane, from where I stood, at the foot of
the Cross, on the Holy Mountain
Who held me tight when my screams rang out, when I felt the pain of that
dark day and watched him again as he walked away
His head bowed down, laden with shame

But this time I did not feel the pain, I prayed to Our Lady to please forgive
him, for I knew it was my turn to hold out my hand
Because Our Lady was with me since my life began
Don't live in the shadow of someone's wrong doing,
Reach out and let Our Lady through, she's standing there, right beside you.

Quote: Forgiveness is the key to freedom.

The Answer

Things in life may sometimes get you down
As the dark clouds seem to gather up above
The moon and stars look as if they have lost their shine
And no one seems to want to share your love

Don't let that sorrow linger one more day
Or keep carrying that heavy load around
For there's a little place that's not so far away
Where all the answers to your questions can be found

Just close your eyes and wonder back
To where it all began
When you were so contented
As a baby in your mother's arms
That piece of mind can be regained
If you would only start
To take refuge with the one that loves you most
Who's living right there in your heart

Just tell him all your troubles and you'll find
He will listen to every single word you say

And he will gently ease that burden on your mind
Then the dark clouds, they will slowly fade away

Quote: If a thousand people were to sit down around a table and write out
all their problems
And pass them around to each other, they would gladly walk out the door
with their own.

Maggie Heston
August 2008

Stand Out

What is it that makes her stand out?
From the rest of her family that she loves so much
Maybe she views life in a different way, guiding her siblings to this day
The love in her heart for her parents so true
Good deeds for them she always would do
What makes her home so full of life, from early morning to late at night?
Is it the stray cat asleep on the chair or the young people with so many
problems to bear?
What draws people to her smiling face?
How do they know about her saving grace?
I think she knew early in life, that she would be different
And always stand out
The price she pays for her healing ways
Would always bring misery and hurt her way
But she took this in her stride
All she could see was the beauty hidden within
And if you were to seek her advice, she would tell you to reach deep inside
Work on the Love, not the Pride.

Quote: Never judge the book by its cover.

Maggie Heston
3 August 2010

Silent Night

Silent Night, Holy night,
All is calm, all is bright
This beautiful hymn, 1818, the year it was first heard
At midnight mass, St Nicholas's Church in Oberndorf
Fr Joseph Mohr, guitar in hand, sang so passionately to the congregation
And they in turn soon joined in
With tears in their eyes and love in their hearts
Remembering the King, the world had, and lost
To keep us safely, in the hands of God

From that little church in Austria
The news of the hymn spread near and far
Once a year, all around the world
In one hundred and eighty languages

This heartfelt hymn can be heard
Father Joseph must look down from the Heavens with pride
For the world is at peace on Christmas night
Singing his hymn, Silent Night.

No matter what war we fight on this earth, there is only one true battle.
Good versus Evil.

Maggie Heston
November 2010

The Fields of Barley

Maggie Heston
26 November 2010

Back in the 1920s the Tans tried to rule our land,
And our people, they did suffer under the English government.

Brave Irish men were shot down, as the women screamed out
'Go on home, British soldiers! For we will not bow down
And if you look around you, then surely you will see, you cannot tame the breeze in the field of barley.'

Those strong Irish soldiers, you'll find that you cannot break
So take your guns and shoot them down, but their freedom you will not take.

All the young rebels who perished for our freedom did not die in vain, for they saved our precious country from the hands of the British rein.

And always remember, their blood flows freely down through you and me.
And their memory will live forever in the fields of barley.

As for the so-called treaties, who are the governments trying to fool, for part
of our country is still under British rule.
Now the rest, they have decided, comes under the EU.

So stand up and be counted, raise the tricolour high,
Never let the memory of our brave soldiers die.

Quote: sometimes man's definition of enough is a little bit more. God gave
us all our own space.
Why would we want someone else's?

The Bearded Man

The piercing stare from his dark brown eyes
Looked across the table at me
Galloping thoughts in his racing brain
Was the man he was looking at, really me!

Or was it a mirror vision of him
Who got his kicks from whiskey and gin?
Or maybe from fooling the public eye
Or thinking about things like pie in the sky.

To unravel the mystery that lies behind every man
Is not by looking at the palm of his hand
Or through rose tinted glasses placed over your eyes
But to really find out what lies behind that guise
For there's a truth to be found behind every mask
And a heart of gold that sometimes beats to fast
And wisdom sufficient inside his head
To help many others that are looking to be led
When he dropped his disguise, it was proved to be true
The real man stepped out with a different view
And the peace he was looking for came at last
With lots of people now taking his path

Now if it is freedom you're looking to find
Follow his footsteps one day at a time
He's changed my life I haven't forgot
For the man across the table was Matthew Talbot

Quote: Like many others, the pain Matt Talbolt carried in his life was to help
        heal others, and the healing continues to this day.

Maggie Heston
August 2010

There's Nothing the Matter with Me

Maggie Heston
15 February 2010

There's nothing the matter with me, I'm as healthy as I can be.
I have arthritis in both my knees.
My pulse is weak, my blood is thin, sure I'm awfully well for the shape I'm in.
Supports stockings I have to wear, or I wouldn't be able to get out of my chair.
Sleep has denied me night after night, but in the morning, sure, I feel all right.
My memory is failing, my head's in a spin, sure I'm awfully well for the shape I'm in.
Ah how do I know my youth is all spent, well my get up and go has got up and went.
I really don't mind I think with a grin, of all the good places my get up has been, sure I'm awfully well for the shape I'm in.
Each morning as I dust off my wits, I read the paper to check the 'obits'.
If my name is not there, I know I'm not dead, so I have a full Irish and go back to bed.
A hearty dinner in the afternoon, then a stroll to the local to kill the time.
Enjoying the crack over a glass of wine, sure I'm awfully well for the shape I'm in.

Remember that old person could be your mum, dad, granny, granddad, aunt, uncle, brother, sister old age is in front of us all. Treat other the way would like to be treated ones self.

The Brew and You

Maggie Heston
20 June 2010

Many a young man got caught in the trap,
The pint of Guinness, the women and the craic
The lure of the top shelf, the music and song, the late night take out, sure it
didn't seem wrong!
Into the morning, the party went on, and when the brew ran out, so did the song
Back to the pub later that day, to get the cure and send the shakes away
Sure, Paddy was there and Biddy too, Ah! Have another one, what harm
can it do?
Twenty years down the line, that same old man is the village clown and if
you take heed,
Listen to what he has to say, I can guarantee, you will change your ways
For what you will find, on the high bar stool, is a lifetime of heartache and a
degree titled village fool
It is the hardest degree you will ever get, so spread the story, not the regrets
And if like him, you're lonely too, you will not find happiness in a glass of
brew

Be tender with your words today for tomorrow you may have to eat them.

Campfire Memories

The lines across the old man's face, so many stories to be told.
Of all those happy carefree days living on the roads.
Happy children, smiling faces as our wagons rolled along.
Stopping where we wanted, with no destination planned.
The friends we made along the way, they were more than just a few.
The farmers working in the fields, their horses we did shoe.
And the meals they cooked upon their stoves, with our kittles, pots and pans.
Every deal was signed and sealed, with a strong shake of the hand.
Take me back to the good old days, when we were wild and free, we had
music in the morning as the birds sang in the trees.
The horses grazed contently on the sweet grass beside the road.
Quenched their thirst from the mountain stream, kept them strong for their
heavy loads.
The sparks from the campfires lit the sky at night, and the stars came out to
play.
Barney on the banjo, with Rosie singing Galway Bay, it was the nearest thing
to Heaven, nowhere else I'd rather be.
And we kept our spirits up with a glass of the old poteen.
It wasn't all plain sailing, the truth I have to say.
A big fat lip and the odd black eye were the order of the day.
There was no judge or jury then, to say who was right or wrong.
For we settled all our differences with a good bare knuckle fight.

Now things have changed from way back then, we had to settle down.
Signing on the dotted line, in the settled people's towns.
But we're not used to boundaries, time will tell you see, we will be hitching
our wagons once again and roam wild and free.
Now there are rules and regulations that do not fit our plan.
Those who give the orders, they just don't understand.
We all have different cultures, the long acre it is mine, and there will be no
more class distinction when we meet our God above.

Maggie Heston
26 April 2009

With education and religion, it is like we are all part of a club.
We may not always attend but can always come back because we are all
members.
When it comes to discrimination, who made the rules?
God made us all, and he also gave us our own space.
Who are we to say how other people should live their lives?

What Went Wrong

Maggie Heston
7 May 2010

Why does it all start out so well, what's your name, gee, you're looking swell
May I take you to dinner, maybe a show
That's how it begins, that's how it goes

A couple of months down the line, getting to know each other, all is fine.
I know your secrets, you know mine
The relationship matures, like a very fine wine
Making plans, the future looks good
Joint-account mortgage, wedding bells

The big day over, the reality sets in
The love is now shared with the twins
Working hard, running the home, rearing the family
Why, oh why does it all go wrong?

Out of the courtroom, married no more, two hearts shattered
A family no more
Why couldn't we see what went wrong?

A shared glance, a loving touch, the secret words, I love you so much
Remembering what we found in each other at the very start makes a lifetime
of memories and two happy hearts.

Quote: A bird in the hand is worth two in the bush.
We never miss the water until the well runs dry.

Peggy the Pig

We rushed out to meet Dad, wondering what surprise he had for us in the basket on the handlebars of his bike; we were hoping for Rolos and spud crisps. Suddenly a little snout stuck its head out of a bag, it was a little pig!

We were afraid and cautious of the little creature, we didn't realise it was just as afraid of us. She was quickly taken into the heart of our family. Soon wherever we were going, she would pursue.

She enjoyed joining in the rough and tumble world of a family of eleven fun-loving children. We didn't know of television, Nintendo, or PlayStation; this little pig was the centre of our attention. She didn't need batteries, made very funny sounds and actions, and befriended us all in her own way. She very quickly became family member number twelve.

Days took on a different routine, my mother had competition! Our little pig would call at the back door to wake us for school, she had her breakfast as reward, (well, we were sure she called to wake us!) travel with us to school, giving the smaller ones a lift on the way there, much to the amazement of neighbours and friends. None of our school friends had such a smart and helpful little pig. She turned for home at the same spot every day and would be waiting for us at the same place every day after school. She became an expert footballer, and we always wondered if there was a possibility of getting her to ride a bike. Her personality shone through, we spent a long time debating her name, imagine eleven of us, and each one of us had our own name chosen and very valid reasons why it was the right one!

In our very first act of family democracy, we all agreed on the name, it was to be Peggy, short for Maggie, meaning pearl, and she was a pearl. We had a party, and Peggy was christened. We were never fully sure what Peggy made of all the debates and the party, but she continued to wake us, come to school, play games with us, and stand back and watch our antics.

Like every child, we thought it would last forever, we will never forget the day we'd seen Mr Sweeney passing us on our way home from school, we all knew the job he used do for the neighbours. Peggy was not in the usual place to meet us. Without saying a word, we rushed for home, too afraid to say anything.

Our worse fears were realised when we entered the shed; there was our friend and pet Peggy, hanging on a hook, slit from top to bottom with the blood draining into a bucket; we were too late to save her, even though we knew there was nothing we could have done.

We were a farming family; there was never any shelter from the hard facts of livestock on farms. The fate of our ducks, chickens, and lambs was never kept secret from us, but there was something about Peggy that had touched us all. We chose to think of Peggy as our companion and friend. I think she also chose us. Her life of three years was short but hopefully enjoyable. We knew that our parents worked hard to support us and would never dare to argue with them.

But Peggy was our friend, and we couldn't accept her fate without doing something! As Mr Sweeney was to find out, eleven carefully aimed stones met him as he pedalled back down the road after his horrible deed. It was our form of revenge.

Days later, when our mother left some parcels on the table for us to give to the neighbours, we all knew what the parcels contained. Each of us took a parcel and left the house, our lonely procession headed for the sandy banks; all thoughts of the neighbours were gone, we could only think of our recently departed friend.

We dug a grave for each parcel, erected crosses, and said our prayers; we prayed that Peggy would be happy.

Weeks later, we did notice that our mother and father seemed to have a slightly strained relationship with the neighbours. Being young, we didn't take much notice of 'some people have no thanks,' 'wouldn't you think that they would say thanks?'
With the personality that my mother has, the strained relationship didn't last long. She soon asked some of the neighbours if they liked the parcels of bacon she had given them, when she was informed that they never received the parcels, there was another lonely procession heading for the sandy banks, this time it was the same eleven but not at a funeral pace!

We ran at breakneck speed! We even passed out our dog Ruby who was blissfully unaware of the emotions that come to boiling point when our mother gets mad! And the amazing speeds she can achieve on her bicycle!

There were many more prayers said on the windswept sandy banks as we removed the crosses and wondered what our fate would be.

Many years later, being grown up and having families of our own, we often discuss Peggy and the effect she had on all of us. How our parents reared us and how we guide our children. Some of us are still reluctant to eat bacon; when we look at bacon on supermarket shelves, memories of our childhood experience come flooding back and our fateful friend Peggy, what she taught us about life, companionship, and friendship.

Peggy was a focal point in our childhood; we are now able to look at the relationship with child and animal on a farm. Being reared on a small farm in the west of Ireland prepared us for life far better than the expensive education of many other more privileged children. We learnt about basic survival, the hard work needed to make a good living, and the need for honesty, love, and loyalty. We knew at an early age what it was like to lose someone close, how to grieve for that person, even if it were a hen, cat, dog, or a pig!

Our small farm was a miniature world with its happiness, problems, jealousies, anger, and grief. For example, to hand-rear chicks and find that a fox steal them during the night, to love a dog knowing it would die, to care for a pig knowing it would be dinner some day. This was and still is the order of life; we accepted this order and realised that it did not hinder or stop us from caring for others.

Staying close to nature teaches us the basic foundation in caring.

If we could all take our childhood education into our adulthood and use it as our template, the world would be a better place. Adults seem to get caught in an intricate web of their own making, the need for money, to have higher status than colleagues/neighbours, and have more possessions.

The Basic Foundation of Caring Is Nature

Many children nowadays do not benefit from this simple learning experience. They are showered with gadgets, software, and other toys that are designed to draw their attention. They grow up not knowing what it is like to look after a sick puppy or lamb; they are able to order burgers and chicken nuggets with absolutely no knowledge of where they came from. They don't know the order of life, what the food chain is, what food is, or how lucky we are to have water to drink.

It is a parent's responsibility to ensure that their children have the chance to see nature for itself.

To know nature is to see nature.

Danaher's Bar

You can ramble in night or day
Just for one, but I'm sure you will stay
Harry, the guv'nor behind the bar
Will serve you a pint and join you for a jar
Talking about times, old and new
While Helena will cook you, the best Irish stew
The locals sitting, on high bar stools
Will fill you with wisdom and throw in a joke or two
The musicians arrive, one by one
With music, songs, and stories to entertain everyone
The clock on the wall might not tell you at all
But sure, you won't be thrown out, 'cos Harry's about
Your name's in the book, the key in the door
A warm bed, could you ask for more!
A hearty breakfast to start your day
Sure, it's very hard to get away
Squire Danaher is calling out to you, 'Have a break, what harm can it do?'
Sit down, have a rest, Harry will take care of you, sure, he's one of the best!

Maggie Heston
6 November 2010

The Road

It started out with so much love,
Carefree, happy, strutting-out stuff.
Feelings inside, sometimes told him that this love was wrong,
Betrowed to other people, pushing these worries aside,
Pretending our gut feelings were right.

Helping each other on life's way.
Hoping our work would not lead us astray.
Poetry and music, that is what we do.
In our weak times, looking for others to lead us to.
Knowing our lady was guiding our way,
For sure in our hearts, believing she will not lead us astray.
Put to the test, may seem the hardest way,
But there's a lesson to be learnt, in our wayward ways.
For good advice to others we cannot give, unless the road in life teaches us,
at will.

The journey to night, I travelled alone.
My mind wandering back, wondering what I did wrong.

Praying to Our Lady, that he would come along, to help me piece together
the love that seems to be gone.
Car after car passed me by, not one of the drivers blinked an eye.
The road was dark, windy, and wet, but I kept on walking in the direction I
was led.
Just as I reached my lowest ebb, a car pulled up, the passenger said:
'Can we give you a lift, sure girl you're all wet?'
Bending down and looking into her eyes, I said:
'Thank you, young girl, I'm fine, because I'm safely led.'

The best teachers in life are on the road.
The lesson I learnt, on this cold winter's night,
Our Lady will always guide us when we are looking to be led
Dear Lady, I pray to you this very night, guide me safely home tonight.
Guide the man that I love too. For he is lost and all confused.

Maggie Heston

Every person we meet in our life, there is always a reason. Good, bad, or indifferent, no matter what the experience brings. There is a lesson to be learnt. This is what gives us the strength to carry on.

Earth's Angels

There is a reason, many don't understand why, God parted them at birth.
He took one straight to heaven.
He left the other one here on earth.
From the bondage of his wheelchair, sometimes restricted to just a smile,
In harmony with his angel brother,
They have changed so many lives

For every year, from far and near, people looking for peace of mind
Are inspired by Thomas and Adam to visit Our Lady's shrine
Some can't walk, some can't talk, and some can't hear or see.
By visiting this holy shrine, pilgrims soon realise their wealth and leave all their troubles behind in Medugorje.

The reason why God chose these angelic twins was to inspire pilgrims to travel to this beautiful land for one week of happiness and a little peace of mind.
Earth Angel Thomas, the inspiration behind the Thomasadam Charity.
Heaven's Angel Adam, with his little friends, descends upon our group and travels with us annually to that beautiful valley, protecting all of us on this special journey.

Maggie Heston

December 2010

Thomas, you will always be in my heart, the years I worked with you as your SnA are among the happiest in my working life. You are an inspiration, and to Adam, thank you for guiding us.

The Thomasadam Medugorje Pilgrimage

What do they do?

In 2003, Maggie Ahern accompanied her mother on pilgrimage to Medugorje. She took with her the feeding bottle of Thomas Scott, a three-year-old severely disabled boy whom she helped care for. The bottle was given to her by Thomas's mother, who requested that it be left at one of the holy sites in Medugorje and a prayer be said for him. Thomas had just been fitted with an intravenous feeding tube and would no longer need the bottle. His parents and extended family were very concerned about how Thomas would cope. Thomas had had a difficult time for such a small child, his twin brother Adam had died at birth, and he had a 95 percent disability. Every day was a struggle for Thomas and his family.

As Maggie left the bottle at the Blue Cross Mountain Shrine and prayed for Thomas, she got the idea to bring Thomas to Medugorje, and he might experience the energy and feeling of well-being she got there.

On returning home, Maggie told Thomas's parents that she would raise the money for Thomas to go to Medugorje; they were delighted and were willing to pay for their own travel arrangements. Maggie got some friends together and set about fundraising to raise €1,000 for Thomas's fare and accommodation.

Much to everyone's surprise, the first function raised €3,000, Maggie decided to continue fundraising and take more children. She founded the Thomasadam Charity and organised the fundraising. Over €20,000 was raised the first year, and twenty-two special needs children were taken on pilgrimage to Medugorje with Maggie as group leader.

The problems associated with the care of so many special needs children are immense but multiplied many times when you transport them to the other side of Europe.

A team of trained special needs carers was formed, the services of Doctor Gerry Cowley were offered, Fr Declan O Carroll and Fr Eddie Rogan volunteered to travel as spiritual guides, Marty Murray, Gerry Flanagan, and Danny Ward offered their musical skills. No detail was missed; the hotel in Medugorje was examined to ensure its suitability for wheelchair access. The airline was contacted to check their policy on children with special needs.

The first pilgrimage was a great success; all the pilgrims found the energy and feeling of well-being that Maggie experienced and were determined to return.

The fundraising and pilgrimages have continued since then, and hundreds of people have had the Medugorje experience.

When someone nominates a child to go to Medugorje and the child/young adult is accepted by the charity, the fundraising machinery moves into that child's area and organises some event: a 10 km walk, pub night, auction, raffles, etc. to raise the fund for the child's expenses. If surplus money is raised, a place is offered to another child from the area.

In addition to the described fundraising, a number of bigger events supplement the account, such as the sponsored barefoot climbs of the Holy Mountains in Croatia and Croagh Patrick and sponsored Christmas swim and bungee jump.

The Charity hopes to continue its work for many years and welcomes anyone that wishes to travel to Medugorje, nominate a child/young adult, or wants to help with sponsorship in anyway.

For further information, contact Maggie on 00353 87 2210849
Or Jackie on 00353 87 1687602
Email: thomasadamcharity@gmail.com

Anyone that wishes to make a donation to the Charity can do so at the Castlebar Credit Union, part proceeds from this book will be donated to the Thomasadam Charity.

No Encore

Please St. Peter, don't take me through,
I've got to go back, there's so much for me to do.
I didn't say goodbye to the ones I love,
I'm not ready to go, they are not ready to cope.
Look, St. Peter, at the state of the Earth,
And look what's happening in the land of my birth,
Our own true faith is falling apart.
God's Words are not being heard.
Everybody too busy tearing each other apart,
Striving for riches, not listening to their own hearts.
Family life slowly becoming a farce,
Morals and values totally lost.
Politicians playing God, calling the people their own flock.
Lie after lie been swallowed up, free will taken by the stoke of a pen,
With wrong information from dishonest men.
Slaughter of the innocence about to begin,
For sure God will punish this deadly sin.
All parties following suit, are they afraid to stand for the truth,
Believing their governments will give them the boot.
Unemployment and poverty all over the land,
Emigration also seem to be part of their plan.
Belief in our country, a thing of the past,
Out of touch with God, it's ever so sad.
Please, St. Peter, ask God to let me go back,
If He grants this request, I promise you this,
I will try to help people out of the abyss.
And what I will try to teach the world,
Is to please, please listen to the truth in God's Words.

Maggie Heston
25 December 2011

It's not what we take with us when we go,
It's the legacy we leave behind.
There are no pockets in a shroud,
No tow bar on a hearse,
And no attorney to shout our defence out loud.
For the only one who can judge us, has the last word.

A Mother's Prayers Answered

Twinkle, twinkle little star
How I wonder what you are
These words kept ringing in her ears,
As she reminisced back through the years.
Off her little girls first angel smile
On her first tentative steps of thousands of miles
Hoping and praying her path would be straight,
But she wasn't to know her little girl's faith.

She fell in love, at just sixteen,
with a boy who would answer all her dreams.
Blinded by her teenage love,
He took her to the seedy world.
Her mother prayed hard every night,
That she'd turn back and see the light.
She taught she was loved by one and all,
Showered with gifts of money and gold.

Every night at half past nine,
She'd dawn her clothes before prying eyes.
Fistful's of money thrown on the floor,
How could any girl ask for more?
Then one night a man walked in,
A kind-faced, bearded gentleman,
He ambled slowly to the stage,
And whispered something in her ear.
Everyone there looked so surprised,
As the tears welled up in her sad blue eyes.
She grabbed her clothes and ran for the door,
And never went back there anymore.

No one knew what the kind man said,
God loves you too were his soft-spoken words.
No one had seen that man before,
Or ever again when he walked out the door.

But something's telling me it was the man upstairs,
An answer to her mother's prayers.

Twinkle, twinkle little star,
Now you're safe, back where you are.

18 July 2012

This story was told in Medugorje passed on by the mother who never gave
up her belief in God's power.
Thank you, Gerry, in turning this into a beautiful song, and please, God, it
will inspire people never to give up on prayer. Only God knows when and
how our prayers will be answered.
There's an old saying 'There is a book inside in every one of us and beautiful
stories to be told, stand up and be counted.'

Breaking the Chain

Everything happens for a reason
Sometimes people come into your life
And you know right away this was meant to be.
They come along to serve some sort of purpose,
Teach you a lesson, or help you figure out who you are,
or whom you want to become.
When you lock eyes with these people,
In that very moment, your life will take on a new meaning.
Changes will happen to you at this time,
That cannot be explained.
You will start to question others and yourself.
It will be like taken a ride on a rollercoaster,
You will experience all sorts of different emotions.
And that person you locked eyes with,
You may blame for turning your life upside down.
On reflection, you will come to realise
The turbulence this person brought into your life,
Actually helped you realise your own potential.
Everything happens for a reason,
Nothing happens by chance or by means of luck.
Illness, sorrow, love, lost moments of true greatness,
Or sheer stupidity, all occur to test the limits of your soul.
Without these small tests,
Life would be like a smoothly paved,
Straight flat road to nowhere.
Safe and comfortable, but dull and boring.
The people you meet affect your life whether good, bad, or indifferent.
The successes and the downfalls that you experience,
Can help create who you are, and the bad experiences can be learnt from.
If someone hurts you, betrays you, or breaks your heart,
Forgive them because they have helped you learn about
Trust and the importance of being cautious.
If someone loves you, love them back unconditionally,
Not only because they love you but also they are teaching you to love
And open your eyes to the little things that matters.
Remember nobody can give you true happiness

They can add to it, they can subtract from it,
Only you can strive to achieve it.
Make every day count, appreciate every little thing,
For you may never get the chance to experience it again.
Talk to people whom you have never talked to before,
Learn to actually listen; give to people, by giving you are receiving.
Break free from old habits, by breaking the chain you are setting yourself free.
Set your sights high, believe in what you are doing.
Hold your head up high because you have ever right to.
Trust, trust in yourself, trust in others, for trust is the foundation of true friendship,
And trust is the only foundation in true love.
Tell yourself you are a great individual
And believe in the same.
Remember amongst the billions of people in the world, there will be one,
Who will truly believe in you too.
Crete your life on truth, for it is truth that prevails.
Bury the untruths, for they are nothing but anchors,
Waiting to hold you back and tie you down.
Cherish what you know is yours and you will be cherished also.
Never live in the shadow of others, you are unique.

10 February 2012

For all the generations that came before us,
How many of them got it right?
Have we not learnt from the mistakes of our forefathers,
What some of them got wrong, which one of us has got the strength?
To try and break the chain and try to get it right.
I wonder why Jesus told us the story of the prodigal son.
The quote (the black sheep of the family)
Is judged by all.
The black sheep is the one that leaves the family fold and branches out
His journey may lead him to dark places,
His learning in life may lead others to the brightness.

The Boy

He was sent to my home suffering so deep inside,
Not even a twinkle or spark in his eyes.
Searching around for most of his life,
Wondering why nobody could reach him inside.
His mother so hurt by the man she loved.
To her children words unspoken,
Thinking that she was easing the way, for the ones she loved, not to be led astray.
Their father she hoped would throw away the disguise,
And see the love she had for him through their children's eyes.
She watched her eldest son being led astray,
The darkness in the world, been the order of his day.
When I looked at him through his sad, sad eyes,
I knew this beautiful boy did not live his own life.
For the hurt he carried to his dying day,
Was that of his and others he could not through away,
And he left this world in disarray.

Maggie Heston
18 March 2013

Dedicated to the boy
From the first day you walked into my home, the healing began, for you touched the hearts of everyone there. You may not have found what you were searching for with us, but in sharing your life story with us all, you helped change the direction for those of us who were lost. You did not die in vain; because of you, many lives have been saved. And your prayers continue to heal us all.
May you rest in Our Lady's arms!

This Is My Life

I want to grow into a big oak tree
The little acorn seemed to say
As it came spinning down with the wind
Like an angel from far away
Just as the seed is sown in the womb
It becomes a boy or a girl
The little acorn will land on the soil
And Mother Nature will take its course

But when they're denied the chance to grow
By ways that are not meant to be
By misinformed people who don't want to know
The joys of a family tree
The rustling of leaves in the soft summer's breeze
Or the clutch of a small baby's hand
Are tender moments that can't be replaced
When we interfere with God's plan

Chorus
This is my life and I want to live
We've often heard people say
But the little voices that have gone unheard
Will be talking to you some day
I don't blame you, Mummy, for what happened to me
At the time you were innocent too
But wrongly advised by some people who knew
The harm they were doing to you

The rules that are made by those who think
Of only material gain
Will realise one day that all their false wealth
Will end up in so much pain
Just remember young people who are caught in that trap
And are going through so much despair
That all the little flowers that were picked too soon
Are now blooming in heaven's care

So don't listen to the lie that's being told to you
And disguised in so many ways
But always listen to the truth in the voice
That speaks loudest in your head
So let's all join together in one loud voice
And help break that evil chain
So no more precious lives will be lost
And we'll all have so much to gain

chorus
This is my life and I want to live
We've often heard people say
But the little voices that have gone unheard
Will be talking to you some day
I don't blame you, Mummy, for what happened to me
At the time you were innocent too
But wrongly advised by some people who knew
The harm they were doing to you

(Gerry was inspired to write this song in his return home from Medugorje
and after reading about the Hallocust of abortion)
Thank you, Gerry, for your kind permission in allowing me to give this
beautiful song to the world.
More info
Visit: WWW.GerryFlanagan.org Or email: Gmmpfla1@yahoo.co.uk

Can Someone Tell Me Why?

Oh, how sad I feel tonight,
So stressed and worried about the state of the earth
Third World countries' people die of hunger, thirst
Can anyone tell me why?

Countries waging wars
Earthquakes, landslides, tsunamis,
Floods, Storms, why so many?

Rich countries strive for fame,
Back street Ghetto's, poverty pain.
Skyscrapers built higher and higher,
One track minds craving power.

Living their lives in the fast lane,
Reaching out for riches and gold,
Forgetting how to feed their souls,
Can someone tell me why?

Have we all forgotten what makes us tick
Lies, deception, murders and rapes,
Media throwing bad news in our face.
Governments all joining force,
Making decisions, counting the votes,
What next, perhaps they'll divorce.

Banks all draining dry,
Bouncing money like pie in the sky,
Still nobody can tell me why.

Scientists now playing God,
Pills invented so we won't grow old.
Churches fallen day by day,
People choosing to stay away,
Blaming God for their downfall,
Knocking the Holy script,
Haven a ball.
Can anyone tell me why?

Abortion bill pushed in our face,
One more way of losing grace.
Enhancing the power of the one below,
Confusing people of which way to go,
Can anyone tell me why?

Medical science at its peak,
People dying on the streets,
Money now the new God,
Where is it leaving us all?

Broken families, children lost,
Quick fixes: ALCOHOL
So many lives wiped out one by one,
Suicide claiming the innocent ones,
Why, oh, why can't something be done?

Spring, Summer, Winter, Fall,
Now mixed up like us all
For sure I am not listing now at all
For I know who is to blame for it all.

St. Michael, spread your wings,
The lost souls are doing terrible things.
Blinded by the evil one
Following the path of total destruction
Help us close the door to the darker side,
Open our eyes to the beautiful rays of the sunlight.

Grab the devil by the horns
Place him in front of our loyal king
With his command may the evil one be banished straight to hell
And may his army follow him one by one,
Until the earth is cleansed of all sin.
St. Michael, thank you once again,
For the battle you fought and won way back then.

And all you good people that are still out their
To St. Michael say a prayer
To help him capture the evil slayer.
And once again St. Michael
You will triumph
For every prayer that prayed from the heart
Is joining forces with God in the battle to be fought.
And when you read this, grab your beads
And pray from the heart on bended knees,
For every single prayer our good God needs.

Quote:
For so long wine and caviar were the order of the day
And the roulette wheel kept spinning
And what really matters in life seemed a million miles away.
The tear-filled eyes of the hungry child with no food to pass its lips,
Men walking on the moon, others trying to reach Mars,
The fuller the pockets the emptier the hearts
All the while the wailing cries of the child went unheard,
We let them die alone.
And now we walk the streets of gold,
With no home to call our own.

Maggie Heston
30 July 2013

About the Rosary

The Rosary is the story of the New Testament. Through the beads we follow the life of Mary and Jesus. We follow Mary from the day the Archangel Gabriel came to ask her to become the Mother of Christ to the day she was crowned Queen of Heaven. We follow Jesus from the moment the Holy Spirit came down on Mary, through his childhood, his cruel death on the Cross, the joy of Easter when he rose from the dead to the day he ascended to Heaven in glory. What a story! And it is all true.

Mary waits for your prayers. If you speak to her, she always listens. She is our Mother. When you pray the Rosary, begin by telling Mary what you would like her to use your prayers for—and then think about the stories that are hidden in the beads.

The Rosary is such a tremendously powerful weapon against Satan that armed with the Rosary in our hearts and the beads in our hands, we can even stop wars. If we but knew how powerful this prayer is, we would never want to put the beads down.

The Mysteries of Light

In October 2002 Pope John Paul II added the 'Mysteries of Light' to the Holy Rosary, calling us to pray the Rosary daily for our families—and for world peace.

Christ's Baptism in the Jordan
The spirit descended like a dove on him. And a voice came from heaven, 'You are my son, the beloved; and with you I am well pleased.'

Christ's self-revelation at the marriage of Cana
Jesus changed water into wine, the first of his signs and revealed his glory; and his disciples believed in him.

Christ's proclamation of the kingdom of God with his call to conversion
The time is fulfilled, and the kingdom of God has come near; repent, and believe in the good news.

Christ's Transfiguration
And he was transfigured before them and his face shone like the son and his clothes became dazzling white.

Christ's institution of the Eucharist
He took the bread, gave thanks, broke it, and gave it to them, saying, 'This is my body, which is given for you. Do this in remembrance of me.'

A long-ago poem that had much significance then. God is still there, but the world has become very busy with its minutes. You, one day, the minutes won't matter anymore in this busy world—what then?
So give it a try—'Just for a minute'.

Just for a Minute

I remember when I was only four,
Mother would bring me round to the store,
And just outside the Church she'd stand,
And 'Come in,' she'd say, reaching down for my hand.

Just for a Minute

And when I started going to school,
She'd bring me down every day as a rule,
But first the steps to the Church we'd climb,
And she'd say: We'll go in, you've always got time.

Just for a Minute

Then I got real big, I mean, seven years old,
And I went by myself but was always told:
When you're passing the church, don't forget to call,
And tell Our Lord about lessons and all.

Just for a Minute

And now it's sort of a habit I've got,
In the evening, coming from work,
Though it takes me out of my way a bit,
To slip into Church with my hat and my mitt,

Just for a Minute

But sometimes I see the other fellow
Standing around and I just go yellow.
I pass by the door, but a Voice from within
Seems to say, real sad: 'So you wouldn't come in?'

Just for a Minute

There are things inside of me, bad and good,
That nobody knows and nobody could
Excepting Our Lord, and I like Him to know,
And He helps, when in for a visit I go,

Just for a Minute

He finds it lonesome when nobody comes,
(There are hours upon hours when nobody comes)
And he is pleased when anyone passing by
Stops in (though it's only a little guy).
Just for a Minute
I know what happens when people die,
But I won't be scared, and I'll tell you why
When Our Lord is judging my soul, I feel
He'll remember the times I went in to kneel
Just for a Minute

Quote:
In the busy world we live in today, we never seem to have time for 'just a to-do list'. How many of us are stressed out thinking we never get it right, we never have time, or is it we never give ourselves time. If that be the case, go on, be kind to yourself, and take time out. Next time when you're passing a place of worship, go in 'just for a minute', that is when you will truly have time to be one with God. After all, you do not need to make an appointment. When God made time, he made plenty of it.

Each Step of the Way

If you come with a heart sincere,
And sorrow deep within.
I will forgive you,
My grace will flow
Gone are all stains of sin.
I will send you forth
With the strength of my power,
To do my Holy will.
If you do this for me
And I know you will.
I promise you, with peace your heart I shall fill.
So go forth in my name and do what I say,
You know I'll be with you each step of the way.
When you fall, I am near, when you call, I shall hear.
When you are belittled, do not fear,
For my graces fill your soul.
Just as you are, yes I love you.
My love is constant and true, and I promise you
Each step you take, I'll take that step with you.

Quote: Those who believe and not see are blessed; those who see and don't believe are lost.

Mother Mary Divine

Mary Mother divine
Mary mother of mine
All my sorrows I bring to you
Help me, dear Mother, to see them through
Help me carry my cross day by day
Dear Mother, give me the strength to follow Jesus and God's true way.
All of my family and friends I place in your care,
Trials and tribulations help them to bear
May peace and love be part of their day,
Forgive me, dear Mother, if I shed a tear,
Help us come closer to Your Son,
Drown out all our fears.
Mary, I love you, please answer my prayer.
Mary Mother of mine
Mary Mother Divine
Quote: Love is the greatest gift God gave us; it is also very fragile and needs
to be treated with care and respect.

Maggie Heston
30 July 2013

Saint Michael the Archangel,
defend us in battle.
Be our protection against the wickedness and snares of the devil.
May God rebuke him, we humbly pray;
and do Thou, O Prince of the Heavenly Host,
by the Divine Power of God,
cast into hell Satan and all the evil spirits
who roam throughout the world seeking the ruin of souls.

Ask through Devine intervention of our Lord Jesus Christ, our Lady, the Holy Spirit, all the holy saints and Holy angels to descend upon you/us. Ask St. Michael our protector to take all the evil spirits away from you/us from our families our homes etc. . . . and place them in front of the holy Tabernacle. From there with the aid of St. Michael that God will banish all the evil spirits into the pits of hell. Nevermore for them to roam this Earth. For the ruination of souls.

Pray the Rosary Daily. Pray from the Heart

Devote one hour on Sunday, go to Holy mass.

Every soul that is born God gave a Holy Guardian Angel to watch over and protect us. If you don't ask your Guardian Angel he cannot help you.

God does not intervene with our free will. We are free to choose our own Journey.

That road is made easier when we have belief in God and his Heavenly choir.

If you like the contents of this book don't praise the author Praise God.

Lightning Source UK Ltd.
Milton Keynes UK
UKHW01f1942150618
324326UK00001B/46/P